marianna

D0297437

Hand Rhymes

collected and illustrated by

MARC BROWN

COLLINS

for my son Tucker

Copyright © 1985 by Marc Brown
All rights reserved

ISBN 0 00 195306 0

First published in the United Kingdom by
William Collins Sons & Co Ltd 1985

Printed and bound in Hong Kong
by South China Printing Co

Contents

My Book

 This is my book; it will open wide

To show the pictures that are inside.

 This is my ball, so big and round,

 To toss in the air

 Or roll on the ground.

 Here's my umbrella to keep me dry

 When the raindrops fall

From the cloudy sky.

This is my kitty; just hear her purr

When I'm gently stroking her

Soft, warm fur.

Five Little Babies

 One little baby

 Rocking in a tree.

 Two little babies

 Splashing in the sea.

 Three little babies

 Crawling on the floor.

 Four little babies

 Banging on the door.

 Five little babies

 Playing hide and seek.

Keep your eyes closed tight, now,

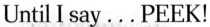 Until I say . . . PEEK!

Two Little Monkeys

 Two little monkeys fighting in bed.

 One fell out and hurt his head.

 The other called the doctor,

And the doctor said,

 "That is what you get for fighting in bed."

Jack-o'-Lantern

I am a pumpkin, big and round.

Once upon a time, I grew on the ground.

Now I have a mouth, two eyes, and a nose.

What are they for, do you suppose?

With a candle inside, shining bright,

I'll be a jack-o'-lantern on Halloween night.

Five Little Goblins

 Five little goblins on a Halloween night

Made a very, very spooky sight.

 The first one danced on his tippy-tip-toes.

 The next one tumbled and bumped his nose.

 The next one jumped high up in the air.

 The next one walked like a fuzzy bear.

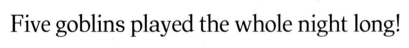 The next one sang a Halloween song.

 Five goblins played the whole night long!

Here Is the Beehive

 Here is the beehive. Where are the bees?

 Hidden away where nobody sees.

 Watch and you'll see them come out of the hive,

 One, two, three, four, five.

 Bzzzzzzz . . . all fly away!

Snowflakes

Merry little snowflakes

Falling through the air,

Resting on the steeple

And the tall trees everywhere,

Covering roofs and fences,

Capping every post,

Covering the hillside

Where we like to coast.

Merry little snowflakes

Do their very best

To make a soft, white blanket

So buds and flowers may rest.

But when the bright spring sunshine

Says it's come to stay,

Those merry little snowflakes

Quickly run away.

The Snowman

Roll him and roll him until he is big.

Roll him until he is fat as a pig.

He has two eyes and a hat on his head.

He'll stand there all night,

While we go to bed.

Little Bunny

There was a little bunny who lived in the wood.

He wiggled his ears as a good bunny should.

He hopped by a squirrel.

He wiggled by a tree.

He hopped by a duck.

And he wiggled by me.

He stared at the squirrel.

He peeked round the tree.

He stared at the duck.

But he winked at me!

Quack! Quack! Quack!

 Five little ducks that I once knew,

 Big ones, little ones, skinny ones, too.

 But the one little duck with the

Feather on his back,

 All he could do was, "Quack! Quack! Quack!"

All he could do was, "Quack! Quack! Quack!"

 Down to the river they would go,

Waddling, waddling, to and fro.

 But the one little duck with the

Feather on his back,

 All he could do was, "Quack! Quack! Quack!"

All he could do was, "Quack! Quack! Quack!"

Up from the river they would come.

 Ho, ho, ho, ho, hum, hum, hum.

 But the one little duck with the

Feather on his back,

 All he could do was, "Quack! Quack! Quack!"

All he could do was, "Quack! Quack! Quack!"

Kittens

Five little kittens

Sleeping on a chair.

One rolled off,

Leaving four there.

Four little kittens,

One climbed a tree

To look in a bird's nest.

Then there were three.

Three little kittens

Wondered what to do.

One saw a mouse.

Then there were two.

Two little kittens

Playing near a wall.

One little kitten

Chased a red ball.

One little kitten

With fur soft as silk,

Left all alone

To drink a dish of milk.

Creeping

Creeping, creeping, creeping,

Comes the little cat.

But bunny with his long ears

Hops like that!

The Caterpillar

 A caterpillar crawled to the top of a tree.

"I think I'll take a nap," said he.

 So—under a leaf he began to creep

 To spin a cocoon;

 Then he fell asleep.

 All winter he slept in his cocoon bed,

Till Spring came along one day and said,

 "Wake up, wake up, little sleepyhead.

Wake up, it's time to get out of bed."

 So—he opened his eyes that sunshiny day.

 Lo! He was a butterfly—and flew away!

The Church

 This is the church,

 This is the steeple.

 Open the doors

 And see all the people!

Marc Brown is the author-illustrator of many books for
children. He says, "I was reintroduced to hand rhymes
through my son Tucker when he was in nursery school, and
they stirred memories of hand rhymes I had known when
I was young. I thought that doing a book of hand rhymes
would be a good way to introduce children to the feeling of
poetry. Initially I collected about three hundred and fifty
rhymes. After whittling down the selection, I devised the
accompanying hand movements." The diagrams he devised
are very simple to follow, making this a delightful book to
share with a child.